Mary Givens

. . . .

ECCLES...

elect

Ever
one

by any
ms, without
te brief

is book but
ned would

Sheffield
City Council

vork.

Renew this item at:
http://library.sheffield.gov.uk
or contact your local library

LIBRARIES, ARCHIVES & INFORMATION

lots of love from Sheffield

by Mary Givens

For my
Auntie Una X

Dear You

Have you ever thought of having a break and working away? You know... getting on a train, boat or plane so that you can have a change of scenery for a while, meet new people, make new friends and generally have a whale of a time.

Lots of us did back in the 80's mostly driven by unemployment, but it wasn't all doom and gloom, people in Sheffield were packing all their cares away and flying around to find work away but not too far from home on the beautiful Channel Islands. I'd like to share with you a few personal letters and photos I received on my travels, whilst working on the channel island of Guernsey in the 80's.

We all had masses of fun, worked multiple jobs, often just to keep our heads a little above water but mostly so we could live (seemingly to my friends anyway) a life of freedom with no boundaries, as we went along playing social butterflies without a care in the world. This was, of course, as anyone has travelled around, and worked abroad, a very far cry from the truth as you will discover!

This book is dedicated to all my friends who are here, in its pages, not one of them really remembers everything that happened back in the 80's and if It wasn't for the letters I discovered, a lot of it would certainly be long forgotten by me too. Without them this little book would not have been possible. ... My friends are now other people's friends too; I hope they make them as happy as they made me.

LOL Mary XXX

I loved putting this book together with my 80's letters and although the letters don't make up a story as such, they give us all a bigger picture of who we were as youngsters growing up in that era.

I tried to contact everyone who had sent me letters back then to get their permission for publication but it simply wasn't possible as there are dozens of letters from friends all over the place, so these letters are my closest to home ones from Sheffield, they are also the most telling intimate ones from that decade.

Some of us were very creative back then and made our own clothes, we were also adventurous, resilient and determined, yet still innocent as to what our lives were to become as we raced or paced ourselves through the 80's.

We all loved to party, a good old session on the drink was never far from our train of thought and going off the rails and letting our mouths run away with us was a regular occurrence.

I always seemed to have my camera on me too, back in the days when it wasn't an app on a phone so I took pictures of us all, wherever we were; well they speak a thousand words too!

A few things I remember clearly, you simply had to have a job and a boyfriend/girlfriend back then and staying in on a Friday or Saturday was never an option. In short, we all loved life!

Me (left) and Lisa B - still best mates today!

. . . .

Contents

Introduction
Welcome to my 1980s' letters!

Introduction

Welcome to My 1980s Letters!

It was Christmas back in 2010 when I first started reading through my old Letters, I hadn't looked at them for at least 30 years, and they go back even further.

It was like discovering an old diary, travelling back in time and looking in at our much younger selves. I was surprised and shocked at what I read, as are all my friends who wrote them as they'd never kept any letters from their past.

I first left home in Sheffield to find work away in Guernsey in 1987 and really that was the strangest thing, reading the letters I'd sent back home, it took me right back to then. I believed the letters could be formed into a book that we could all look back on as kind of a part of our life souvenir. Well, with their permission I've decided to share a few photographs and scribbles with you. According to some letters a few of my friends thought I was living the Life O' Reilly back then, having masses of fun without care in the world, flying backwards and forwards to Sheffield for Christmas and Birthdays so I didn't miss out on too much.

This was, of course, as anyone has travelled and worked away from home a very far cry from the truth as you will discover! These are proper letters b4txt {;) and Social Media. Please enjoy them, and meet my younger friends who wrote them to me... who knows, maybe you know or recognise one of them (some of them are very heavily disguised...) I hope you enjoy reading and reminiscing as much as we loved living it up 80's Stylee...

This is Reality Reading

LOL Mary XXX

(That's Lots of Love in my books!)

Chapter 1
Life without stabilisers

I scribbled my first letter to my Auntie Una in Sheffield at around 5 years old accompanied by a matchstick illustration of myself in crayon riding on my bicycle with no stabilisers, and with a purple/pink sun beaming down on me I was an independent happy bunny.

Two years down the line with no stability in my early years or anyone to play with I'd penned my first letter to Santa, and got the biggest surprise when he wrote back to me! I hadn't even put my name on it so he addressed it to The Young Lady who lives at... well by then I was seven and smitten as he'd even stuck a pretty pink Angel stamp on it which cost him 2 and a half pence.

Out of all the children in the world I had the letter to prove that he really existed, of that I had no doubt. So my love of letters had already begun and a few years later I'd write off anywhere and everywhere just to see if I'd get a reply in return and that included the BBC who replied, and the Tufty club who didn't.

It was in my first year at secondary school when I thought I'd been hard done by after counting out how many wheat crunchies were in a bag I'd bought from the school tuck shop, so I let the manufacturers know all about it and they delighted me a couple of weeks later by sending me a letter of apology and whole box of their products for free! They couldn't have timed it better; I had my friend around after school that day, and she was gobsmacked when she saw what I'd received in the post, a whole box of goodies to get stuck in to after we'd had our tea!

I'd become very confident in my letter writing by the time I'd hit my teens and after an illicit {and illegal} couple of halves with my friend in the Bar Rio in town aged 16, she was attacked on Pinstone Street, so I wrote to The Sheffield Star as though I was her to tell everyone else about it, and again I left my name off in case it was published and my parents saw it. It was published, I was very proud I'd found my feet and the letter writing bug was born.

From Italy to Sheffield
The Tiger Bikini

15th August 1981

Dear Hairy Mary,

Just thought I'd drop few lines to tell you what I've been up to, which is quite a lot I can assure you. I'll start on the journey to get to Itieland.

On the boat we had a laugh because there was a big gang of French boys who kept following me everywhere, and even came up to me while I was sitting with my Mum and Dad! One of them called Alan got all six colours on Adrian's Rubik's Cube! We got through France with no bother, and we drove all through the night and day to do it, and didn't stop till we got through the St Bernard Tunnel, in the Swiss Alps. We stayed in a beautiful hotel, not far from the tunnel in the Alps.

By then I was starving, and had been frying all day in the car, and so I was dying for a bath, but then trouble began in Italy. We started early in the morning, but at around 12 0 clock we got stuck in the biggest traffic jam I have ever seen in my life! It was August the 1st and all the factories had shut, so all the Italians were heading south on the biggest motorway in Italy.

All Saints

There were just too many cars for the road, the policia couldn't do anything about it, but what they did was stop a lot of cars at different points, so that the cars wouldn't run out of petrol by going dead slowly all the time. The weather was really hot, and so everybody including us (who were in the jam) just got out of their cars, and walked around, and played cards and things like that, so if you could have seen us you'd have laughed your head off.

Every so often, a helicopter which everyone thought was the television flew over us, anyway, gradually things got better and we were able to travel continuously at only 40 miles per hour. When we stopped at a service station, it was jam packed with cars and people, and it was then that Dad found out he couldn't close his car door, so we had to tie a rope round the back door to shut it, and then we carried on.

But then we had an accident, What happened was, we were in the third lane when a back tyre just exploded, the car went out of control and we just crashed into the barrier in the middle of the motorway separating the two sides, we were all shaken but not hurt.

We all got out to look at the damage which wasn't as severe as we thought, the left head light was smashed, and the bumper had got bent, and the wire which connects the indicator and headlight and petrol measure

9

had become disconnected, so we had to move to the other side of the road to change the tyre which was hard to do on a motorway but we did it though, and we stopped at a garage to get the indicator wire fixed, and the rest we did when we got here to San Biase.

We arrived here about 2.30 in the morning, and we were very tired. Since I've got here, I've done nothing but kiss people, and my lips are so sore because that's how they greet each other over here. There are some nice lads over here especially one called ****** and ****** got herself a boyfriend called ******. The people here are really friendly, but the girls are all after ****** and all they ever say to me is 'Where's *******?'

But there are some nice ones. When we went to the seaside, we did a rare daft thing. You see, we were swimming in the sea and came across a buoy with a rope attached it, and Adrian was messing about around it and he thought the rope was attached to a boat, and that the boat had got free, he began to panic, and kept telling me to go to the bar to find the life guards, to tell them what had happened.

I had on my Tiger Bikini so when I ran to the bar everybody was looking at me, and I got the woman at the bar out, who told her husband, who told the lifeguards, but they asked me if it was my boat and when I said no they laughed and said 'Well why are you so worried then!'

Then my brother ****** told me that each buoy was attached to each other and the boat was kept still by the anchor – oh boy! Was I shamed, but the lifeguards didn't mind and they kept talking to me, and saying why didn't I stay at the seaside with them (which I wouldn't have minded!) but I had to go home for my dinner.

Another stupid thing I did was just the other day, there was these boys on mopeds whom I knew were from the next village, they were all stood round our car and one of them looked as though he was doing something to it, so I ran up to them and said 'F*** off leave my car alone' it ended up they weren't doing anything (shame and a half) but they kept following me everywhere, but I got rid of them eventually.

I have been to a festa here which wasn't bad, actually there's one tonight here in this village. When we went to the nearest biggest city Campo Basso, I was in heaven, because as I was walking back to Zia's house with her and her family all these Italian police, loads of them, from all directions were walking towards me, corr... it was great, all those uniforms!

Life's been quiet here, except for the other day, when after a wedding here, the bride's sister and hubby had a terrible crash, the people who had been driving behind them took them back to the bar, where the woman got out with blood pouring down her face, screaming hysterically, begging for somebody to take her and her hubby to hospital, everybody was too scared, and said they had no petrol but somebody eventually took them.

The woman had 25 stitches and supposedly lost an eye, the man had got crushed ribs, a broken thigh joint, and lots of lacerations and severe injuries, it was a horrible coincidence that the accident happened right next to the cemetery, I didn't see the woman but ****** and ****** did, and she was so scared she was crying.

There is a fantastic lad here called ******* I even think Mary you would like him. ******** coming home today so you should see her soon. Well, I hope you like the few lines I dropped, and I hope the letter gets back home before I do, but before my pen runs out and I have to fetch it, here's a stupid joke.

There was an English man, an Irish man, and a Scots man and they needed a room for the night so they went to a hotel and asked for three rooms, the manager said he'd got three, but one was filled with ants, another bees', and the other snakes so they took the rooms.

Next morning the Englishman and the Scotsman were all bitten as they had shared the rooms with the bees and the snakes, but the Irish man wasn't bitten at all and he had been sleeping with ants, so they said to him, 'How come you haven't been bitten!' So he said 'Well, I killed one ant and so the rest of them went to the funeral, boom boom'. See ya soon.

Love Zia Bag Beauty, Fried Supreme (The great one).XXX

Mary's letter writing debut

It was never just the postcard from my friends as we travelled around in the 80's, we all sent each other letters, whether we liked it or not, well there was no way we'd have had the cash for a good ole catch-up on the dog and bone, and in the 80's if you were abroad and wanted to use a phone, sometimes you'd even have to involve an operator, or wait to get connected from a phone exchange!

Well, this is one of my favourite letters for so many reasons, the innocence, and the attention to real gory detail... plus I was totally engrossed at the way Italians had such holidays! Life's been quiet here... Really? I dread to think how she'd like to liven things up!

Can you imagine actually hand writing a letter this length though now... on holiday? One thing is for sure though, I wished I was there; it could only happen in the eighties, here we go again with the corny jokes too. Zia bag beauty loved uniforms so much. Wait till you read what she decides to have a go at a few years later.

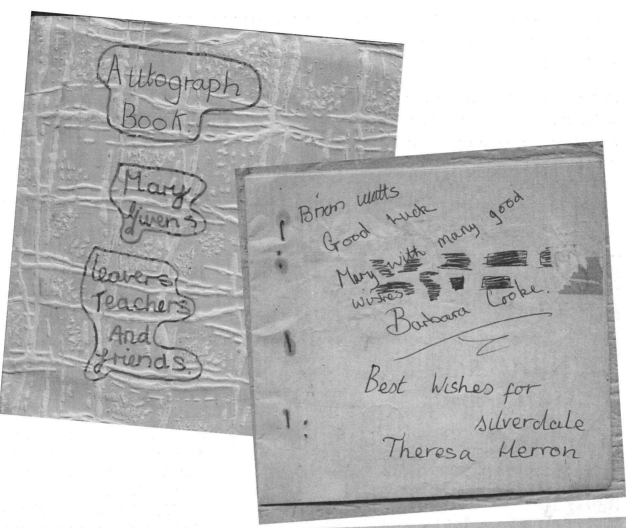

Mary's DIY autograph book

Redgates ESTABLISHED 1857

Your Ref.
Our Ref.
Date

The Young Lady who lives at
245 Meadowhead,
Sheffield.8.

Dear Little Friend,

Thank you for your letter - but you forgot to put your name on it ! I have
written down that you would like Tracey Tea Party, Esmeralda, a Teddy Bear, a
Cooker, a Washer and a record. I will do my best to bring them on Christmas Eve,
but you must promise to be a good girl, and be fast asleep in bed when I come.

Lots of love,

Father Christmas

THE REDGATE CO. (SHEFFIELD) LTD. 18-24 Furnival Gate, Sheffield S1 3LE. Tel: 0742 · 77585.

From Cardiff to Sheffield

Star Date 25-3 81 Marshal of RAF Brooklyn Bryant

Dear **** x Dear Mary x Dear Wooden top x Dear All,

I'm finding it very difficult to address my letters these days. Anyway hope you are all well, yes including you wooden top. You wanted a mention in my letter so you'll get one you horrible snivelling little rat (don't worry, I'm only kidding) hope **** didn't get into too much trouble that Sunday.

Ill just put a few jokes in now because I want a laugh and I haven't got a picture of wooden top. Joke time, mum why does everyone call me count Dracula at school? Shut up son and drink your soup before it clots! Ha ha ha. It's the way I write em, keep incest in the family. Ha ha who is this comedian? Two lepers having a meal, one dropped his fork and bent down to pick it up, So the other one dipped his toast in his neck ha he ha he ha he! But there's more.

Two lepers playing brag one went blind, so the other chucked his hand in. boom boom! No stop I can't take any more oooookkkaaaaaaa ill stop. This is a piece of my mind * don't know why I wrote that, I'm going to bed now, goodnight zizz dream zzzzz zzzzz dream zzzz.

Good morning playmates and how are we today? Well I have two choices here, I can either pack in writing this stupid letter or I can ask **** for some more paper. Guess which decision I made. Anyway, now I can go on writing this trash.

By the way I'm expecting a reply to this letter, with all the style, versatility, and production I've put into this one. You know what I mean write it in the bog or something. ****... **** sends his regards, you'll probably see him before you get this letter, I'm not coming home anymore because nobody loves me * teardrop. Anyway, let me tell you about the good old RAF, I could sum it up in one word, but I don't want to swear.

Food 0 star quality -10

Accommodation 3   star quality -5

Training +10 +10 +10

Seriously though folks, its great stuff, its hard work though. Me and't old lad **** have just finished a 92 hour shift, then after that we had to walk 50 mile back on us hands. Hang on for a moment because my favourite records on... It's gone off now. By the way ****, the next time I come to Sheffield, I'm coming up to the Girls Venture Corps, to see you in your uniform and that goes for the other two... yes!

I want to see you 2 and a 1/2 females (sorry wooden top) in all your glory! Well, better go now, but before I leave, just a few jokes.

What's the difference between The Pope and a Trebor mint? Trebor mints last a little bit longer!

Have you heard about the new German microwave oven? It seats 50! Stop I can't take any more! 'Ok, I will'.

I might see you soon.

Tarra! Marshal of the Royal Air Force (Kojak) Agent Brooklyn Bryant. uc.gc.mbe.cse. Obe.ba.bsc. Ad vd ac sac pbt fo etc...

Ps... I've written 3 letters and you've written 0, and I'm vexed

*Pps... **** sends his regards*

Ppps... I send my regards

Pppps... The whole camp sends their regards

*Ppppps... Its' not true ****

Pppppps... Hello wooden top

Ppppppps... Hello Mary.

*Pppppppps... There will be no more PS's see ya ****.*

Excuse the handwriting, I've got choclera, this letter is contaj, connta, contagax catching.

Beware the seal - it bonds in seconds.

The contents of this letter are fragile.

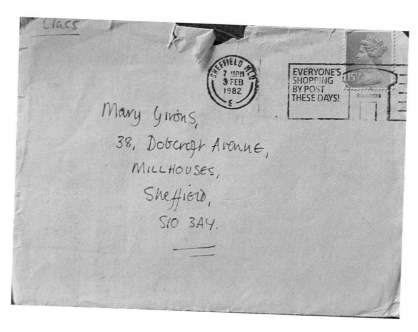

    This Soldier went on to do 8 years in the RAF. We haven't met since but it was mostly the discovery of this letter that got me reading all the rest, It's nothing short of a miracle that I found him again on Facebook , and frightened the life out of him, with a huge blast from the past, he couldn't believe I'd kept this letter for 30 years.   And then I went on a little journey of my own through all my other letters... back to Sheffield... Italy... and Guernsey... 80's Styleee! Please pardon the non PC Jokes too; the 80's were full of them!

Chapter 2

The Apprentice Hairdresser

Hairdressing was the only option I had of getting into college as I wasn't a huge success at studying and my exam results weren't cutting edge enough to do what I'd hoped.

I'd done my two weeks work experience in Rackham's in Sheffield at age 15 and gained lots of experience in picking up dry cleaning for the stylists, I also had my first game of bingo down near the markets at lunchtime lured on by an exotic looking 2nd year improver with purple hair.... we won a dozen eggs between us!

Still, that little stint didn't put me off and my first proper job was at Ciccarellas Barbershop and Ladies salon on Abbeydale Road, sweeping up and brewing up, followed by shampooing and passing up papers and perm rods in the ladies Salon. I had the best start in my working life it was just like one big family at work together and we all had a fantastic social life in and out of the salon.

Christmas Eve was the best when we'd all have a tipple of Sherry or something else seasonal with the customers before 10 in the morning and by 2pm we'd usually be in the Dove and Rainbow enjoying plenty more of the Christmas spirit{s}!

To be a great hairdresser you have to be talented and arty with your hands and imagination, and really I was neither but you can't go wrong with what I felt was the more important side of the job, customer service and chatting away to strangers about their highs and lows and more importantly to me, their holidays.

I'd never been abroad apart from visits to Ireland, but to me that didn't count as you'd have to have arrived back in blighty with a tan and you didn't get one of those after a holiday in Dublin's fair city. Judith Chalmers was all over the telly with tales of travel at that time, and by then I'd started Wishing I was her…

'The boss' - Tony Ciccarella

The Old Blue Bell, High Street

Mary's first Saturday job

Ciccarella's lavatory 'round the back love'

Lunch at Henry's

Lunch in Henry's with Ciccarellas staff and pals

Henry's

Liquid lunch at Henry's

Temptation Guernsey to Sheffield 1987

Dear Mary,

I haven't got your letter yet to tell me what mischief you've been up to. I might phone you up today from work if you're lucky. These were the first words of the letter that was too much for me to bear, my best friend was having a whale of a time over in Guernsey.

Her boyfriend was in the Guernsey American Football Team, and she'd popped over to join him. Her life sounded so exciting and I could have done with a bit of that in my life too, I really loved working at Ciccarellas Hairdressers but I knew there was more to life than footballer's shaggy perms, shampoo and sets, and blue rinses. Her lifestyle was so far removed from mine and I wanted a piece of the action overseas, where food shopping was frozen crispy pancakes from a supermarket called Island Wide, and going out every single night of the week was par for anyone's course.

The maddest thing is though; she was mentioning that Guernsey was full of people looking for and finding work {without too much bother} from Sheffield and all over the UK, and Ireland, even my old school friend, Carmel whom I hadn't seen since we were at All Saints School on Granville Road Back in 1982 was there too with her big brother.

Carmel was working at a Hotel, St Pierre Park and doing a bit of part time in a takeaway called The

Raising a glass to Henry's

Munch Bar where my best mate and her new pals went all the time for Chips and cheese savoury after getting a few bevvies down their necks in a place called 'The Thomas De La Rue' which sounded terribly French and glamourous. Then there was the club scene, Scarlett's was mentioned regularly, as was The Golden Monkey, and whilst going to a club just about every night of the week was a stark reality over in Guernsey; that kind of lifestyle in 80's Sheffield was only in my wildest dreams! She usually finished off her letters with a huge sarcastic remark and even bigger bait like "I'm going to play Monopoly now piglet (from work!).... I'll write again soon, so be good, and if you can't be good be careful (as if!) And start saving!!!

Love from Me to You. XXX

I saved less than £199 but I didn't give a monkeys uncle... My motto was 'I can and I will' and with that I was off!

Ciccarellas

Granville College hairdressing students

Mary and Francesca Ciccarella

My first boss and my second boss - Julie and Susan at Ciccarellas

Trying hats on at Cole Bros

Chalk art from the Hole In The Road

Chapter 3

Welcome to It's a New Life

Looking around for work in Guernsey was an eye opener for me, there seemed to be an abundance of jobs there for the taking if you were willing to put in the graft which of course we all were.

We were all cut from the same cloth over there regardless of where we'd travelled from, and that cloth made up a patchwork cover of all our experiences in relation to unemployment back home wherever that may have been.

Service industry jobs were the main event in the Channel Islands as their own youngsters went into more lucrative businesses such as Banking and the like. It allowed young people without a string of qualifications to follow our dreams and get a decently paid job in shops such as Boots or Benetton, or you could even have a bash at whatever you thought you could turn your hand to, it was very possible get promoted to manager at the drop of a hat after a month or so, all you had to do was prove to the powers that be that you could do it, and the job would be yours…no bother, and all of us without exception worked our socks off.

The local residents of Guernsey are the most welcoming hospitable people, and I have great memories of the kindness I experienced while looking around for places to live, there would always be a local resident to make sure you wouldn't be sleeping under the stars as they would find a spot for you under their own roof, and for that I remain truly grateful.

Guernsey was a melting pot of young Portuguese, Italian, English, Irish, Scottish and Welsh youngsters back in the 80's and all of us gained a priceless lesson in life, we all worked and played together, there was no North/ South divide, and no racism, we were more likely to be sharing our food and drink, our Telly and even our clothing. Guernsey was the best experience to set me off on my working life journey, and it gave me other things no amount of money can buy, belief and confidence.

A new life!

Le Chalet Hotel
Sheffield to Guernsey 1987

Hiya Mary   how's the new life?

Thanks for your letter & menu (pig) it was great to hear from you. Sorry it's taken us so long to write back, but we've not had the time (actually we're idle gits!) We haven't got much to tell you as we lead such boring lives. I told a few of the gents in the barbers the other day that you found a job as a chambermaid , and most of them hope you are making the beds, and not just ruffling them up ha!

At the moment Julie and I are having lunch; we have had a boiled egg and Ryvitas. Guess what, we haven't been to the chip shop or the Butchers for a roast sandwich for 3 whole weeks! Well, enough about us (Told you our lives aren't interesting) how are you and how's the job? Are you still enjoying it? Have you been paid yet? Or have you had to find the Town hall steps? When I phoned your mum, she just couldn't believe that you would make it at 6am every morning. So I hope you have, in fact just wait a moment I'll just phone her and see how she is.

Ok im back, your mum says you phoned on Sunday and everything's fine. So you're working some other jobs as well? It sounds as though you're having to work hard for your money for a change ha ha. Have you found a replacement for Wallis yet? Guess what Julie was desperate and actually let me cut her hair the other day, I couldn't believe it, god knows what it will be like when you get back (if?). Have you met a nice man yet? If so, let us know all about him.

*The Hotel you're at looks really pretty, like something in the Alps. Are the people you work with nice? Do you go out much at night? Has Paula written to you? We haven't seen her at all, I used to see her at the bus stop but I haven't lately I bet she's missing you, we are. My back is really killing me, the Saturdays are still a killer but the bank balance is growing, trouble is, ill probably die before I can spend it! Francesca and Rebecca are fine thanks Julie spent all her birthday money on Rebecca at Asdas so she's ended up with nowt again (poor lass). Here... Mr. Reynolds has just given you a sweet.... Oh, sorry Mary just couldn't get the spice in the envelope so here's the wrapper as a reminder of what your tips used to look like! Good job it wasn't a Mars Bar. ****** has gone on holiday so has Ginny (lucky gits) I suppose you're brown as well, Julie and I are still very pale, every time it's our day off the sun goes in. The weather is crap today and it's quite cold too.*

Le Chalet girls

25

. . . .

Anyway Mary, I will say bye for now, im sorry the letter is not very interesting but write back to us and we will send a better letter next time. We may have more tell you next time after Ginny returns, you never know she may come back engaged, lucky devil has gone to Malta for three weeks. Anyway love, take care and write back soon, say hello to ***** and don't work too hard. Lots of love and all the best

From Citizen Smith xxxxx

PS Julie still hasn't had time to write in this space she will write next time. Hurry up and write back to us XXX

| Boots perfumery Guernsey 'Jaki' | Boots perfumery Guernsey |

My good old hairdressing mates made sure I never forgot my roots! This was the first letter to me, at my new place of work, Le Chalet Hotel, in Fermain Bay a beautiful place in a woodland setting, surrounded by bluebells at that time of year, and I was in love with it. I'd got a job as a chambermaid so I didn't have the bother of finding accommodation as all the staff lived there in a little staff house. I'd done the right thing, I missed them all, but my new life was exciting, and I was meeting people from all over the place. Guernsey was indeed full of people from all over the UK and Sheffield all giving the ball a good hard kick whilst they worked hard but partied even harder!

Waterfront staff   **Boots perfumery and Waterfront staff**

Herm and Champagne, flowers and two irons, insert

From Me to Sheffield

Dear you Guess what,

I've left Le Chalet, and I got a job in boots as a perfume consultant working for Nina Ricci, Worth and Roger and Gallet and I love it, no more getting up at 6.30 to make someone else's bed which was really hard after our nightly staff parties.

I had to find somewhere else to live though and the rent is really expensive over here, you can either live in local market, which is just for residents of Guernsey, then there's staff accommodation (which I just left) or open market which are few and far between. So I needed to share with someone else, well I went down to The Waterfront Restaurant where I eat sometimes and asked some of the staff were they looking to move from their staff house and this Irish girl said yes.

We'd never met before and she's from Cork in Ireland but we get on like mad! We found a place we both like it's a big bedroom with a built in wardrobe sink, a table 3 chairs and a dressing table and two bedside cabinets so I'm landed. The sea is just down the road and town is 10 minutes stagger away. I was lucky to get paid from the hotel after two weeks as I hadn't signed a contract.

I'm starting at Boots on Monday and someone told me I'd be going over to Jersey with this job to attend the perfumery exhibitions and I'm so excited. I don't think I could get used to living in a place with no sea nearby; I'm always going off for a stroll along the beach over here. Last weekend was Liberation day and it

was boiling, it was so busy over here and everyone
was brown walking around St Peter Port, it was more
like being in France. The fair came to town too and
I went on the big wheel with my old school friend
Carmel who works over here too, never again... I
thought all my tomorrows had come at once! I'm
going to the launderette tomorrow it's nice there too,
in a place called The Moorings. I'll send you some
photos as soon as I get them developed if I don't give
them all out again as I usually do!

I'll have to go now and buy some smart clothes for
my new job, I have to wear a skirt, can you believe
it, but at least I'm not wearing Boots blue overalls so
I'm happy about that too.

Take care and see you soon

Lots of love Mary XXX

My counter

Boots perfumery

St Peter Port

Fermain Bay

High Street, Guernsey

Keyhole fashion

Keyhole fashion, full of stone-washed denim

From Ciccarellas to Guernsey
June 1987

Hiya Mary

Hope you're well and still enjoying yourself over there. I phoned the pub two afternoons last week; to see if you were in, but you must have been hard at work for a change. How's the new job? Are you enjoying it?

I didn't think you stick it as a chambermaid for longer than a month; you're more suited to perfumes anyway. Oh, are there any more free samples? That Diva was lovely, and that new Nina Ricci one was nice too.

I saw your Mum and Dad the other day in town, they looked well, your Dad was off for the week, but the weather was terrible, what's it like there? I'll bet it's lovely and hot; your Dad said he could do with a haircut, so I told him to call in.

*Julie and I also told your mum to come down for her hair done but she hasn't up to now. I just thought I would write you a few lines whilst I had the time to, we've been to the nursing home today and I'm really knackered. I must tell you last time we went there ****** was taking one of the women back from the hairdressing room in the wheelchair and when she pushed the chair out of the lift, the woman fell out on the floor, and it was all a bit messy, I know, its really bad isn't it, poor woman, but we had to have a bit of a break after that incident (god aren't we terrible).*

. . . .

The other woman Mrs Bottomley do you remember her? She always tried to take a good bite out of you, if you happened to be giving her a backwash in the sink around lunchtime, and she's always saying 'I want to die' and well, I sometimes wonder if she means it poor lass, lovely though the home is.

Today I had to push a very heavy woman, up a really steep slope in a wheel chair, I couldn't speak when I got to the top, and when I took her back down again we went down the slope around 30 miles per hour, I have never moved so quickly in my life and I was frightened to death of letting go of the chair, or it taking off with me hanging on, it was a bit of a Frank Spencer scene. I don't think we will carry on for much longer; it really knocks you out at the end of the day.

We went out last night to the Pine Grove Country Club it was a first Communion party, ****** had done most of the grub it was really good. ****** Sends her love they make a good couple really don't they... I actually spoke to ****** for a while, wow he's really lovely, mind you he was a little chatty with all the vino, but what the hell, so was I. It's the first time I've been out for ages, and I really enjoyed it. Guess what ****** is going away to work for a week on the 29th of June, we could have had a great night out, but im going to Italy on the 25th so we've got no chance, he timed that one well.

Are you still coming over for a few days if so when? Paula's mum came in for her hair done the other Saturday; she says Paula doesn't go out much at all. Do you write to Paula...? Well im sorry I haven't much to tell you ****** is having another baby on the 1st of Aug and she only told her mother in law yesterday. It was ****** birthday the other day she had a party at Cairo Jax, and ****** went and got off with one of her friends, she lives in a dream world that one, I asked how many were going to the party and she said 80 but ****** said there were about 20 if that. Anyway love, that's all the scandal for now, sorry about the writing, but I'm falling asleep, I'll send you a card from Italy, write back soon.

Lots of love Citizen Smith.

So, I'd had enough already. Big respect for anyone who can make up someone else's bed for a living, the early mornings were a killer after mad parties in the staff house, and the starched sheets ripped my hands to shreds. I'd seen a job in the Guernsey Press for a French speaking perfume consultant, so I said my Au Revoirs to all my new friends and off I trotted.

A cuppa before the start of work at the Waterfront

La Fiorentina

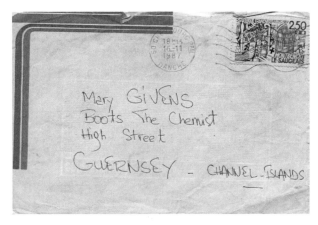

Mary GIVENS
Boots The Chemist
High Street
GUERNSEY — CHANNEL ISLANDS

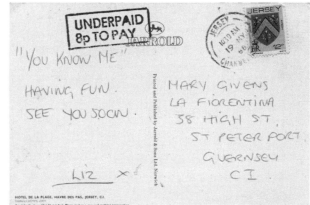

UNDERPAID
8p TO PAY

"YOU KNOW ME"

HAVING FUN.

SEE YOU SOON.

Liz x

MARY GIVENS
LA FIORENTINA
38 HIGH ST.
ST PETER PORT
GUERNSEY
C I.

Le Chalet

Location: St Martins (Fermain Bay) • Guests: 80 • Hotel register: ★★★ AA ★★★

Le Chalet nestles in a wooded valley above picturesque Fermain Bay which is one of the most beautiful spots on Guernsey. The hotel has access to the beach, which is about 250m away downhill and runs a regular, complimentary minibus service into St Peter Port.

Quality country hotel, set in delightful surroundings • Traditional breakfast • Four course evening meal • Cocktail and lounge bar • Indoor swim spa, jacuzzi and sauna • Sun terrace • Car parking • 40 rooms en-suite with heating, hairdryer, tv, telephone and tea/coffee making facilities • Open all year round.

LE CHALET				BOARD: B&B	
Code: G2415	SEA- Portsmouth		AIR- Gatwick		EXTRA NIGHT
No. of Nights	3	7	3	7	
1 Nov- 15 Dec	246	370	271	394	44
1 Jan- 27 Feb	246	376	271	394	44
28 Feb- 30 Mar	258	391	271	415	44
31 Mar- 26 May	283	443	308	468	56
27 May- 30 Jun	312	479	336	503	58
1 Jul- 31 Aug	312	485	336	506	58
1 Sep- 30 Sep	298	462	322	475	58
1 Oct- 31 Oct	266	395	305	419	54
1 Nov- 15 Dec	246	370	271	394	44

Supplements per person per night: Half board payable locally, Gold from £3, Platinum room from £7.50, Gold Single from £7.50.
Children: 0-1 year free by Sea or £50 by Air plus 12.75 per night. 2-11 years 50% reduction.

Flexible durations available from 2 nights or more.
* From prices are to be used as a guide and can fluctuate especially during peak periods. See page 4 for what's included in holiday prices.

Added Value

FREE NIGHTS (B&B)

For every stay of 5 nights receive the 5th night free.
(10 nights = 2 nights free)
Valid 01 Apr to 30 Apr & 01 Oct to 31 Oct

For every stay of 7 nights receive the 7th night free.
(14 nights = 2 nights free)
Valid 01 May to 30 Sep

For every stay of 4 nights receive the 4th night free.
nights = 2 nights free, 12 nights = 3 nights free)
lid 01 Nov to 15 Dec 10, 03 Jan to 31 Mar & 01
y to 15 Dec 11.

Guernsey

To book visit your local travel agent, call 0844

prestonholidays.co.uk

57

Just get your letter love the perfume
A K Nick

MISS M GIVENS
LA FIORENTINA
38 HIGH STREET
ST. PETER PORT
GUERNSEY
C.I.

HELLO MR POSTMAN

DON'T YOU THINK IT'S A COOL STAMP

Guernsey life

From Sheffield to Guernsey
1987

Hiya Mary

Thanks for the letter; I got it Wednesday like you said. I'm really glad everything's turned out for you, it sounds great over there, the only thing is, you seem to have lost your magic touch with not having a bloke and all that, ha ha only joking!

*Well, from your letter you're definitely having a better and more exciting life than me. I've only been out 3 times. On wed 3rd April, just went down to the Wagon and Horses with Mum, Dad and Nan, not too many in (thank god) Then Nan took me out on Friday 11th May and you'll never guess where to? Yes, you got it in one Wagon and Horses (again) Nan kept getting me gee and tea and by 9.30 I'd gone (Gone with the wind ha!) well you know what I'm like with a few drinks down me, I only went to the phone box and rang ****** up, he answered it, I couldn't think what to say, so put the phone down (hope to god he never finds out it was me!)*

*Then Tuesday 5th May went to the best place in Sheffield yes you've guessed it again, Woodseats - went with ****** just went in all the usual hot spots Chantry, Big Tree and Abbey which was like grab a granny so that speaks for itself really, so back to the Big Tree to see if ***** was out but I couldn't find him, good job really, cos id had too much to drink by then and my mouth would have run away with me!. Anyway Later on in there 3 blokes came over and talked to us, ****** ****** and ****** they were called, anyway ****** had a car so they took us out to Dronfield for a couple, (it was ok) then they took us out for a Chinese and ate it back at mine, they stayed until 1.30 and ****** asked me out (he's the one you wouldn't look twice at) I might just let him take me out once just to take up some spare time. Are you missing the curry and rice at night?*

*Well, besides going out drinking 3 nights I've still managed to keep riding my bike, well I've only been twice, once on Monday 27th April and only up to Totley with ****, we stopped off at Nan's for a drink and a cig then on Thursday 30th April I put the clock forward at work so I got home 15 mins earlier I didn't bother having my tea, and instead I wrote a letter to ****** (I've put a copy in for you to read what do you think about it woman of the world?) and called round for ****** on the bike, then just messed round in Mill-houses Park with ****** Plant till it went dark, then me and ****** made our way up the Grove and we know who lives up there don't we? Well you might have forgotten, so I'll remind you, ******! It didn't take me long to find his house and I had the shock of my life, it looks really big and posh, anyway I didn't have the guts to post the letter so I got round ****** to do it, you wouldn't believe what she did; she only knocked on the door! But luck was on my side for once, no one was in. So she put it in their letter box. Well, up to now he hasn't been in touch, so I've made up my mind that I'm going to be a good girl and wait for him with fingers and legs crossed and we'll see.*

Everyone says Hi and look after yourself, went to see your Mum and Dad last week, they're ok, and I paid some club money. Hope you like the photos I sent you, I haven't sent the negatives on, cos im having some copies done of (nudge nudge) you know who. Went to the dentist last week and he told me I've got to go back 14th July and have both front teeth capped you'll never believe how much its going to cost ! £33- each tooth

- Dad said not to go back, instead he's going to take me to the dental hospital, so I'll let you know how I go on. My teeth are slowly coming white now I brush them 6 times a day without fail. Saw a couple of your old mates the other day (I nearly forgot) they were going into Henrys, but I didn't say anything.

Bye for now, take care and I'll write again next week ok!

Love Paula XXX

Me at La Fiorentina (home)

Twin beds at La Fiorentina

'Room mates' at La Fiorentina

From Sheffield to Guernsey
1988

Dear Hairy Mary,

How's tricks oh jet setting woman? So you're still over in Guernsey? Have you met the man of your dreams yet? Or are you having a bit of a nightmare with it?

Apparently Paula thought you had gone missing about 4 weeks ago, I think she was going to send out the RAF out for you and the lot, but that Big Momma of mine told me you rang me, so I know you haven't been kidnapped\abducted, or carried off to a faraway land. I can't believe I missed you when you came over, did you hide or something eh? When is it you are coming to Sheffield again? You just let me know and ill make sure im not here! (Tee hee) No only kidding, tell me now so I can arrange things, you know what I mean, and inform that fiancé of mine and stuff, and we can have fun together okay!

Well, things are pretty much the same here with work and all that but guess what, my Mum and Dad are on holiday, and im "Having the time of my life" it's like a holiday in paradise for me (well maybe that's going a bit far, after all, I am still in Sheffield!) No more of Mums nagging for 2 whole weeks', I'll think I've gone deaf! ****** has suddenly turned our house into a free hotel 'Hotel Italiano' I call it, you never know who is sleeping there from one day to the next. The other day I found my cousin sleeping in my bed, and you'll never guess what, he had a plastic bag over the pillow because I had a cold sore and he said he didn't want to catch it! Cheeky. So I've been sleeping at MY new house, you'll have to see it as soon as you come back.

Me and my lover have set another date again, it's in June on a Sunday, so book it in your diary jet setter, and mosey on down here. I might even allow you to come to the buffet as long as nobody sees you, and you wear a brown paper bag over your head ha ha, only kidding again! Mary, I haven't been to a nightclub for 2 zillion year, can you believe it? Well actually it's probably about two months if I work it out properly. I'd been poorly you see, and running myself down working at the restaurant, but hopefully later on tonight I'll be boogying on down at poserfines, I wish you were here to boogie on down with me as well, with your Madonna sunglasses, jumping from one side of the dance floor to the other with a John Travolta look alike.

Anyway Mary, write soon and be a good girl... like me ha ha.

Lots of love, The one, the only Zia Bag Beauty, Fried Supreme.

PS. What do you call a rabbit with a bent knob......?

(I think I've told you this)

The answer is F****S Funny. Get it F****S Funny -- Hope you laughed or you're dead meat.

Guernsey to Sheffield 1987
Me to You

Hello you, how's things in Sunny Sheffield?

I'm still enjoying my job on the perfume counter and I've taken on another one in the evenings, I'm waitressing in a restaurant called The Waterfront and that means I can get into the Golden Monkey nightclub for free, because it's downstairs.

I'll never be able to stay in now! Next month a few of us are going over to Jersey to watch some American football We're going on a tiny plane where you have to move the seats to get on, and you can talk to the pilot too. Today it's not very sunny so I decided to write some letters.

The other day an old lady came up to me and asked how much allowance of perfume she could take back home with her, so when I told her it was 250ml she bought a big bottle of Opium for £54 and had it all poured into squeezy bottles so she could dodge the customs, and she didn't want the lovely empty bottle either so she gave it to her friend who seemed very happy. Perfume here is very cheap so I'm buying you a bottle of Chanel no 5 and I'll bring it over to you, aren't I kind!

I'm happy with the little miniature bottles and sometimes if something is discontinued we get a free tester. Paula is coming over soon so I've asked my landlady (who gets drunk a lot) if she could stay in my room and she said yes so that will save her some money. I hope she likes it here, it's the first time she'll be going on a plane as well. Well all my pals at the hairdressers said I'd be back in Sheffield after two weeks and I'm here two months already with no regrets and three jobs instead!

I love the shops here there's a fab shop next door that sells really beautiful ideas for presents, things like hand stitched silk scarves, gorgeous handbags and Belgian chocolates, all I need now is the boyfriend ha ha. We all went out to a restaurant called Friends the other night, there's always a great atmosphere in there and we have takeaways too because we can't cook at home. Well I'm off now I have to go upstairs to someone else's room to watch the telly, If Tomorrow Comes is on. Oh listen to this I nearly forgot, there's a pub across the road from us called The Jamaica Inn, and someone told me that Oliver Reed goes in there, I'd love to bump into him, I bet he's a right laugh.

Take care and lots of love

Mary XXX

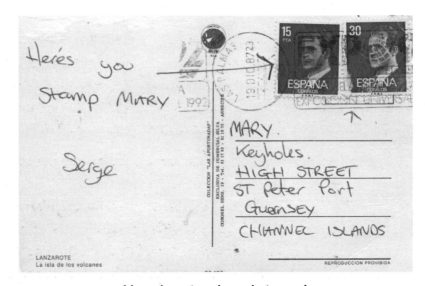

I loved postcards and stamps!

Beautiful Channel Island

La Fiorentina, St Peter Port to Sheffield

Hello you

Well I trust you are well. I am thank you very much I'm getting a TV on Friday so ill be settled for life then, EastEnders omnibus on a Sunday and Coronation Street and all that, I haven't watched them for absolutely ages.

I told the supervisor at work that I was thinking of going home at Christmas and she seemed to think I wasn't entitled to any holidays, but my boss says that I am, so I told the supervisor that if I wasn't allowed any time off, id hand my notice in the week before Christmas, and she wasn't so hasty then. They know what its like to try and get staff in that shop, so it's tough on them.

I don't really enjoy working there so much anymore because it's very boring... at first it was like a challenge to see if I could use my brain as well as my hands and work with figures and stock books, and now the job is too straight forward and simple, and I want to move on to something else a bit more challenging. I like working with perfumes, in fact I wouldn't mind making a career out of it. Id like to be a travelling rep – working for a Perfume House such as Chanel, Christian Dior, or YSL and going around all the perfumeries in the Channel Islands and promoting their goods there's lots more paperwork to do but also lots to see while travelling. We have different reps in our shop every week and they really enjoy their jobs, so I'll just keep my ears open and hope something turns up.

It used to be so embarrassing though, when customers came up to me and asked me for perfume (In French sometimes, so I've had to dust a few cobwebs away) but I've managed to waffle through it. Oh, I served The Emmanuel's with perfume the other day, Rive Gauche by YSL (They did Diana's dress) Well I have just woken up; I didn't work in the Waterfront tonight because I was too tired, it is now 11. 20 at night and I dropped off at 8 o clock. Tomorrow (my day off) im working in Keyhole fashion, and I've started filling shelves here in the evening so I can get my full staff discount.

On Saturday im working down at the tent in ST PETER PORT because it's powerboat week, and Boots have got a stand there so ill get to see a few races and I hope, you get to watch it on TV. I haven't had a chance to see the Yachts' yet, but I've been told they're just out of this world. How's Timmie... is he still missing me? Aah-hh. It's coming to the end of the season now, so everything is getting quiet you can tell because the nightclub downstairs from The Waterfront (THE GOLDEN MONKEY) is getting quiet on Monday nights and usually they're full by 10 - 15 and you'd have a job to get in. I get in free so I usually go there instead of my usual place which is full of Portuguese. The other nightclub is downstairs from the Old Government House hotel I think that must be the best hotel on the island. ****** has gone out tonight because her friend from Cork is over, this place is full of Irish people about 7 staff in our shop are Irish and I've met a few people from Sheffield too! Which is really funny. I'll have to send you some photos of this room. It's quite nice but not as good or big as the first place in La Cigale. Our room is painted pale green and the curtains are dusky pink so we're getting quilt covers in pink and green to match, and a lamp shade so it will look nice, and then a couple of plants and we'll be landed. I think I'll send you some gift vouchers from Boots and you can get something from Sheffield for your birthday, and ill bring you some jewellery over for Christmas ok? I put a skirt away in Next today, so im getting that on Saturday, its wool and expensive about £36 I think, but I like buying nice stuff while im here.

Room 4 staff house

My weekly expenditure has been reduced, because we live in town, and I don't have to pay for taxis anymore unless I go to other nightclubs but that's only once a week anyway, my food is taken off my wage at the Waterfront and I don't pay to get into two clubs. I get free travel on a little boat to Herm which is lovely for a Sunday out and a picnic. I can't wait to come home for a bit, I bet ill find Sheffield really dirty now compared to here where the streets and everything are spotless.

When my friend's Mum and Dad came, we went to the Butterfly Farm, it was really nice, there's a big conservatory as a restaurant and another conservatory for the butterflies, but we didn't go in because we were going to watch an American football game, and running late, so we just had our lunch and went to the match. I'd like to work in Jersey or France next year, im leaving here in April as far as I know, and I don't really know what I want to do yet though, I'd be ok if I got a job in Rackham's or somewhere doing what im doing now. I was going to go for a job working for Christian Dior, but I don't like the area manager she's a right bitch, the girl who used to work for them in our shop had to go home to the Mainland but everyone says I shouldn't be put off by the boss, plus I wouldn't have to do training again when I got home if a job with Dior came up so I might do that next year.

I don't know though, I'd have to make people up and everything, and some people expect miracles!! Im going to start buying pressies next week and packing them in my case. I really can't wait to get on that plane you know, I like it here and there's no hassle but ill think im in the lap of luxury when I get home! Actually I've surprised myself at how organised I am im quite tidy YES TIDY! I do my laundry regularly and I can iron and even make a proper bed (Thanks to my 5* training in Le Chalet) I can make a Knickerbocker glory, Cappuccino with lovely frothy milk and a marvellous Peach Melba (Thanks to my training in The Waterfront) in fact I think I can turn my hand to do absolutely anything now! Im looking forward to seeing ****** and ****** I bet they've grown quite a bit and I'll bet ****** is still dieting, they've only written me two letters but they phoned up when I was working with ****** in the shop on my days off. Well this address is semi permanent now, its open market accommodation so I can properly unpack my case and put my stuff around me, and you can write to me here.

The room is £55 a week between two of us the landlord must be a millionaire because he owns the restaurant downstairs as well, and that's a really posh Italian. Richard Baker the news reader was in our restaurant last night and Liz served him he was with his wife and mother and Mike Reed the Radio 1 DJ was in last week and I saw The Crankies on the bus as well! So we get to see a few famous faces, there should be a few over this week for the powerboat racing. Did Auntie get her letter? I hope she writes back I love to receive letters from people, ill have to write to Lisa as well. Well im going back to sleep now, its 10 past 1 ill phone you soon, take care (isn't it funny how I always manage to write 8 pages) this pen refill didn't last as long as the first one mind, and im on my third one now.

I still love garlic bread and I've eaten that many jacket potatoes and pizzas that I ought to look like one! Im missing mashed potatoes though and I wish I had a kitchen but im thankful for what I've got now. Oh at the Waterfront when it starts to get dark we light candles and put them on the tables and I always light one for you, miss you and Timmie.

Lots of love and kisses. Mary xxx

Very pale everytime its our day off the sun goes in. The weather is crap today its quite cold now. Anyway Mary I will say Good-bye for now I'm sorry the letter is not very interesting but please write back to us and we will send a better letter

Boots perfumery

HOPE I haven't bored you too much?

(HA HA)

JOKE OK MARZ. (JOKE)

Just a little reminder of what it Looks like

SHEFFIELD!

Le Chalet Hotel
(LE HOTEL.)
MISS MARY GIVENS GIBBONS
FERMAIN BAY (STAFF HOUSE)
GUERNSEY.
CI

PHILOSOPHIÆ NATURALIS PRINCIPIA MATHEMATICA
Sir ISAAC NEWTON (1642-1727)

Love the apple stamp

From New York to Guernsey

WE always kept in touch us lot working away. Even if you were lucky enough to fly away for a weekend you would send a postcard. Well, some of us were luckier (and richer) than others. This card came all the way from New York to La Fiorentina on the High Street in Guernsey she'd already started her next life journey and left us all behind where we lived like poultry, ate like pigs, and partied like animals with one bathroom per 10 rooms and at least two people per room ......

Hello wee Hens (She's Scottish, just in case you were wondering)...

Its lil wee hen here and im fine I hope you are too. Sorry I missed you before I went, it was so rushed; anyway I hope you forgive me. Its good here im definitely staying on In camp America, im only 2 hours away from Manhattan. Anyway keep in touch I miss seeing all your faces and Mary did you throw out that milk? Keep on drinking the Diamond Whites (or blush if they've run out of white again!)

Take care see yous' sometime.

Love wee hen. XXX

What I would have given for txt msgs after that milk incident. It would have been so easy to txt thro out mlk from Guernsey airport instead of wondering for two whole weeks where the manky smell was coming from, and for the stench to curdle its way up two flights of stairs, meander through the corridors and do a stinky slinky under the landlords front door. We never saw each other again.

Chapter 4

PMT Holidays

Passport, Money and Tickets and you're ready for take-off. My friend Paula had a ball in Guernsey and Jersey, and to be honest with you I did too. We visited places I'd never been to as my work schedule kept me in St Peter Port.

I saw Guernsey through fresh eyes and looking back at the pics I don't know how we fitted everything in with me working full time. We bussed it all over the place visiting lots of tourist attractions I'd never given a second thought to. The Little Chapel was my favourite discovery, such a beautiful tiny place adorned entirely with seashells and fragments of pottery that held a fragment of Guernsey history during the German occupation. It was immaculate and I was amazed that no one had added their opinion in graffiti.

Paula was over the moon with the nightlife too as everywhere was within staggering distance, pubs, clubs and takeaways too, and if you needed a cab to go anywhere else after all that, it would be there in a squiffy jiffy!

Jersey was the place to be on a Sunday, you could get a bevvy there in any pub without having the bother of eating anything as you'd have to over in Guernsey due to their licensing laws back then, and although clubbing in Guernsey on a Sunday wouldn't be possible, come nightfall in Jersey back in the 80's you could go to a nightclub …. But you weren't allowed to dance!!!

That didn't bother us one iota as we would have been in no fit state for dancing after a session in St Heliers finest drinking establishments, where you would see photos galore of

Guernsey bus shelter - PMT Paula's holiday

'Bergerac' played by John Nettles and filmed in Jersey. Paula never got on another plane after her return home; she was and still is a proper Sheffield Homebird…good on her!

From Sheffield to Guernsey

Hiya Mary

Just a few lines to let you know that im alive and well and that I've got my passport, money and tickets at the ready. I've got my case all packed, so all I'm waiting for now is the plane, I've been ready since I bought my ticket on Monday so I hope you believe I'm coming over now. Mum said she'll believe I've gone when I'm on the plane!

Dads' going to take me to the airport, you'll never believe what time, 6.30 in the morning at East Midlands Airport! That's so that he can get back early, and go and do a job, I'm going to be walking round like a zombie, so have some Gin ready to revive me ok! I can't wait to see you all dressed up in your perfume counter posh clothes, and you'll be wearing a skirt too! I never thought I'd see you with your legs out... im going to take some photos and show them round the Wagon for everyone to have a laugh...! Only kidding.

Sorry to hear you haven't got any of my letters, but you move all over the place and I can't keep up. I hope that when I come over you will have somewhere for me to get some kip while you work. I've not been doing anything exciting, well I have, but I can't write it down in case this letter goes astray, and I can't tell you on the phone, cos there's always someone there to listen in. So I'll tell you everything Friday night, and I'm going to make your eyes pop out. Got in a sticky situation on Saturday night, it was meant to be a laugh at first but it ended up in a frigging nightmare for me so enough said.

*My sex life is nil now, well it wasn't up to much before ha ha. I haven't seen ****** for about three weeks now; she's still with her beau so her sex life must be ok. Our bruv had a good holiday with the sounds of it; he*

said he's glad you like the post-card (eh?) Hi from lil sis, she's in love again, and she sends you her spare kisses the cheeky cow. Mary, let me know where to go when I get off the plane ok. I know you can't leave work to pick me up, so I'll just come to the shop and find the perfume counter with my case when I get there ok? I'm writing off now cos I've got to get some overtime done. Be seeing you soon I can't wait, and it's my first time on a plane... scary, but exciting!

Tarra

Love Paula xx

Friday night out, Guernsey style in the '80s

PMT Paula's holiday

Sheffield to Guernsey 1988

Hi Mary

Thanks for the letter, it was great to hear from you, didn't think you'd write so soon. Anyway, nothing much been happening over here at sunny Sheffield if you can call it sunny, you've got to be joking! got up this morning to see about 3 feet of snow (GREAT FOR SNOWMEN!) Yes, I've been out Friday night, down London road, and the business later to Locarno got chatted up by this div of a lad whose name I can't remember, along with total memory loss of what we talked about! Oh, I do remember him going on about bloody football I think, so I just walked off and went on the dance floor, cos if I'd stayed any longer I'd have poured my pint over his head. Anyway when I went back to the bar for a top up he'd gone, thank god.

Overlaid Saturday morning for an hour, so of course I was late for work, don't give a toss anymore every time someone says something to me at work, I give them a piece of my mind, they don't say much back ill tell you. Went to Locarno again Saturday night ****** and ****** were there with the slag bags, they kept walking over to where we were standing, and a couple of times ****** and I looked at each other, but I looked away first. God, every time I see ****** I am in agony I want him so bad! ****** is still mad on his mate too, and on Saturday night she had a bit too much to drink and she was talking to one of his mates. Well, she told him everything (shame or what) how much they should be together and the works. I didn't know where to put my face, and then she only let her gob really run away with her when she told him all about what went on with that other mong from Worksop. Oh well, it's her life what can I do about it.

Well, this weekend they're all in for a surprise im going to nickname myself wild child just hope I'll have the guts and be able to live up to it! I'll just pretend I'm you ha ha (sorry). Thursday had to take Pebble to the vets for a jab, I came home in tears cause it was the first time I'd been there since Cindy got killed, I've got over it now, but im never going again. To top everything off, that night I had a phone call from ****** he'd only gone through half the phone book to find my number; anyway I said I'd give him a ticket for my 21st (you know when you wished you hadn't?) He's nice enough if there's nothing else worth gawping at but he's not my type really. Anyway he only asked me out (NEVER) and I didn't know what to say (well I did know, but didn't want to be too blunt!) so I told him that I'd got back with my X boyfriend Saturday night (wishfully thinking) So I think I nipped that one in the bud.

So Robbie had left Guernsey when you got back from Jersey had he? Oh well, he must have got the hint when you stayed out all weekend partying in Jersey, they don't wait around forever you know Mary. I bet you're really upset as well aren't you, boo hoo. Well anyway I think you're more suited to scouse ******! You're a bit dry with your humour and he's still wet behind the ears bless him!! Say Hi from me anyway. If only I'd got £300 quid spare I'd send it over to you and ****** to get your arses over here for my 21st but I'd be pushed to find £30 right now, so all I can do is have a few drinks to absent friends ok! Everyone sends their love and to take care. Say Hi to all my new Guernsey mates for me.

Bye for now and lots a love Paula XXX

PS: Why friends are like knickers? ~ some crawl up your arse ~ some snap under pressure ~ some don't have the strength to hold you in ~ some new ones get into the crack a little sideways ~ some are your favourites ~ some are cheap ~ and some are ~ Well just plain nasty ~ and when push comes to shove some actually do cover your arse when you need them to!

PMT Paula's holiday

PMT Paula's holiday

'Life's a beach and it's all mine'

Aurigny Airlines for channel hopping!

Sheffield to Guernsey 1987

Hiya Mary

Happy birthday! How's everything going on? Have you settled down ok in your new place? Sorry I haven't written for a bit, but I've been making a jacket and got into a right bleedin mess, and I've been having to occupy ***** in between (know what I mean!). Don't get the wrong idea about him, its not serious... well not on my part it isn't. Well, come to think of it when I have been serious it's only been with *****.

I keep seeing him around without HER but they are still living together. If only I could get him alone for just about an hour or so, I could give him a taste of what he's missing, and I'm sure he would come back to me but it seems it'll always be wishful thinking. I haven't been out on London road (well not on a Saturday night) for six weeks now. It must be because I know I can't play the field, now that I've got Steve. I can't just piss him off yet, because I've got him under the thumb. Last Sunday Mum and Dad took us all out to Bridlington to see my granddad, he's down there on holiday, we only went for the day, and we all enjoyed it (but its not as good as where you are) By the way Dads sold the Datsun we had, and now we've got a white Maestro, its really nice, my bruvs been driving it everywhere and anywhere but he hasn't got his test till 4th Nov 87. I haven't driven it yet cos Dad won't let me, not until I've had 4 or 5 lessons.

So when I do pass my test, I've suggested that I'll be able to drive down and see you and everyone! Well wouldn't that be fun, we could have a big orgy at ******* place, she'd really enjoy that! (Only kidding) When you ring me up or write, I just feel like packing everything in and coming over, but I've settled down at home now. The first week I was back, I promised myself I wouldn't settle down, but now I just have to see what happens. Saw **** on Thursday and gave her your new address, so she can write to you ok? Going out tomorrow night for bruvs birthday up to Woodseats, The Big tree and The Chantry and all that I hope it's a good night. I will write next week some time ok? And I will ring you up at the Keyhole Boutique on Thursday 1st Oct 87 if you're still working there on your days off.

Please say Hiya to everyone at La Cigale and tell those scouse mates of yours' to stop nicking Mrs McGuire's tins of soup she's not daft you know, it doesn't matter how many G+Ts she's had at tea time.

Tarra for now. Love Paula.xxx

Sheffield to Guernsey 1988

Dear Mary, Mungo, and Midge alias Mary the jetsetter.

Believe it or not I have actually put pen to paper and I'm writing you a nice letter. What happened to you the other weekend young lady? I never saw you once you naughty girl, I couldn't believe it when I heard you had come over for Paula's 21st what happened to you at the party, did I hear you met some nice chaps or something? I hope your friend **** enjoyed her stay, god knows how though in sunny Sheffield. How's tricks then? When are you coming over again? It's my birthday next week!! Ha ha. Its bloody windy here again, I bet if I grabbed on to a kite I could fly over and see you! I hope I don't get blown over like you did!

I'm afraid Terri's love life is no longer working; she's flown the love nest cos her lover upset her. Guess what he did right, he said:

'I've got something nice for you'.

And she said

'What?'

Then guess what he did, he only farted, so that's the end of their torrid affair.

I can't wait for all the millions of valentine cards I'll be getting on Sunday, mum's put aside the living room for them all, and the postman has got a crane ready! I've nearly got all my uniform for a Special Police Constable so from now on it'll be Zia Bag Beauty here reporting and taking down all your credentials! Me and my man are still madly in love we're going to Majorca in May cos I got the flight for £29! I saw the offer on the telly, so much for America hey! Everything's much the same here except what I have told you. I've been in touch with ****** lately and she wrote a letter to me, and you'll never guess what the whole letter was about, yes her dog ,about how much it costs to feed it and how much its' tablets cost, so when you write back to me, I don't want to know about any animals OK! So write soon baboon, and a warning! Never ever enter Sheffield again without visiting me, or the punishment is death by tickling!

Love from luscious Zia Bag Beauty. XXX

Paula's holiday

From Sheffield to Guernsey

Hiya Mary,

How's things going? Thanks for the photos, every time I look at them I remember what a great time I had (ha ha wink wink) There's nothing much to write about, but I'll try not to make this letter too boring ok?

*So, I haven't been out to a nightclub for 7 weeks (boring cow) Last Saturday ****** met me after work and we just went looking round town, but didn't buy anything. You'll never guess who I saw In the pub, only ****** with his girlfriend well, we saw each other straight away, he gave me one of his sexy smiles and a sly wink, but she saw him and gave me a look to kill, well, I couldn't have cared less, so I smiled back, just for a laugh, ****** wanted to know who he was and how do I know him? So I told him a bit more than he needed to know for good measure, with a huge pinch of salt just to make it worth listening to.*

Must have added a bit too much seasoning though, cos he got a right mardy face on, and you'll never believe it, he only left me in the middle of town so I had a couple of halves in the Pig and Whistle and got the 17 bus home. Anyway he rang me up when I got home and HE said sorry, anyway that night we went to Fanny's we got there at 11 and the rest of the gang got turned away at 12 cos it was too full so they went to Locarno.

*Well, I got bladdered and had a whale of a time but I don't think ****** did, cos I didn't talk to him much and he still had the face on over ****** I couldn't have cared less if he went and got off with someone else. I had to sleep at his house though, because I'd spent all my money and he'd only got enough taxi money to get to his house. Nothing happened though; I fell asleep as soon as my head hit the pillow. From this Saturday we are having a weeks break from each other (my idea) up to now I've stayed in still making that jacket I told you about and I should have it finished for Christmas!*

*Well I've got some really good news! Well it is for me, but I know you'll be pleased for me too. I don't know if it's true only what I've heard. ****** and ***** aren't living together they've finished. So I'm going up to see his Mum, I'm going to take her that post card I never sent her, and I'll give her one of those fans. Don't you think it's a good excuse to see if ****** is back home? (Fingers crossed everything is true.)*

*I did ring you up on Thurs at the Keyhole Boutique and someone told me you'd gone, anyway I left a message and hope you got it. Well Mary, I've had my hair cut up at the Terminus and they cut it into a bob, the entire perm is out now and it looks ok. Everyone sends their love as usual; we all miss you and look after yourself. Well I've got to go now and get some more cover notes done or I might just get the sack! Say Hi to everyone for me especially ******.*

Bye for now love Paula .XXX

Ps. have you got another guy yet? Take care ok xx

Paula with a Guernsey cow

Sheffield to Guernsey

HIYA Mary

*Got your letter Friday morning, and I couldn't believe that you were ill! I hope you are ok by the time you receive this letter. I haven't been to work at all this week cos I've had the flu. Everyone seems to have got it or had it, I must have been sympathising with you! I'll be back at work Monday morning though, full of the joys of winter (ha ha). It's one thirty in the morning and I can't get to sleep, I've got so much to tell you, and I thought I'd better write it down before I forget anything, so here goes. I did go and see Mrs. ******and she was really pleased to see me, we had a really long chat about this and that and yes, ****** was there looking great as ever (home for good) didn't know what to say or do, my heart was beating that loud he must have heard it.*

Well, he broke the ice first and we got on really good, it just felt like old times, but I had to open my big mouth as usual and asked if he was still seeing that cow, and the answer was of course yes, well... that was that, and we didn't have much to say to each other after that. I could have screamed my head off there and then. So, the only thing he told me afterwards was that he is getting done for drinking and driving. Well his Mum insisted he drive me home winking at me at the same time. I told him to drop me off at the Wagon and Horses cos I know if id stayed in that car any longer, I would have made a fool of myself, and told him I still wanted him and would have him back any time.

*I haven't seen him around since that day. Well, like you said I know it's not like me to keep anyone hanging on, but I haven't got anyone to go out with. ****** is still with ****** and he still doesn't trust her to go out drinking with me but I couldn't care less. Im going to finish with ****** anyway on Sunday night, but only after he's took me out, I'll let you know how it goes anyway, then I'll be free and I can do what I want to do without asking anyone, I'll just tell him in a sweet voice to bog off (after last orders). Oh my god, I saw ****** at the chippy the other day, she's got her hair permed and she looks just like a bloody poodle, anyway she told me that everything is off, her engagement and the lot, but I couldn't be bothered to listen to all the gory details.*

*Hey guess what! You'll never believe who's left his wife, only ****** from the pub! I nearly choked on my cig when I heard, but its not surprising really, she's had three kids in four years and he can't even hold down a job, and I've seen him down in Josephine's trying to chat up the bunnies behind the bar the idiot! I saw ****** yesterday and he's off to the army on Wednesday, we'll just have to hope this will make a man of him! Ha ha.*

Thursday night we had a storm, you must have heard it or read about it, nothing bad happened around here but it hit London bad. Well Mary, you'll just have to believe me when I say I haven't been out for 8 weeks to a night club, I just can't be bothered to get ready, I've got the staying in bug, the only trouble is, I stay in but don't seem to be saving any money. This Tuesday 20-10-87 everyone is going on a do with the Wagon and Horses, it's being held somewhere in Barnsley, I'll let you know how it all goes ok? Lil sis was crying the other day she was heartbroken with growing up pains and I felt really sorry for her, I've even bought her a new pair of shoes she's wanted for ages just to cheer her up. (They cost me an arm and a leg from Dolcis) She keeps saying she'll pay me back (NO WAY) bless her. I've got my fingers crossed she gets over whatever it is sooner rather than later. (Been keeping my fingers crossed a lot just a lately don't you think). I've nearly finished that jacket off; hopefully I'll be able to wear it for that Wagon do.

Thanks a lot for the photos, they are great, love the one of sexy eyes, been drooling over it for days now. Ill send you some photos over soon ok... By the way I've sent off for my driving license if I get it back in time I'll be having my first lesson on the 1st Nov. lil sis says it's a fate worse than death anyone out on the road that day, she's got a cheek anyway, she's like a crazy mad woman when she's let behind the wheel. I can't wait for Christmas to come, you'll be back and we'll have a whale of a time.

I'm going to start saving for the nuts and all the trimmings!! Im going to stop writing now and I hope I haven't forgotten to tell you anything, its turning light outside now, so I have to get some sleep. All the family and Pebble say Hello, and to take care of yourself. Bye for now and see you soon,

Love Paula. XXX

The Little chapel

Chapter 5

Photoshoot Sheffield

Dear Sheffield

Thank you for not being by the sea,

Otherwise I'd never have left you!

Out on the town - '80s style

The Locarno

Smokin' cigars in the Millhouses

Chubbys!

Paula's birthday

Paula's 21st, 1988

Paula & Lisa H - best mates

Air travel in the 1980s

'Poseurfines - staff and customers outings were a regular occurrence

May '84

Three writers in this book

'80s hair by Natalie & Davina - Benidorm 1985, my first 'foreign holiday'

Millhouses pub in the 80's with spin the wheel in the background

Two ladies and a man in black

When all else failed the Locarno was always an option on London Road

Christmas

Me and Paula - two nuts with all the trimmings

'So This Is Christmas' (Sheffield) - 'out for a ruby murray'

Chubby's in the '80s - in a basket!

Fancy dress December '85

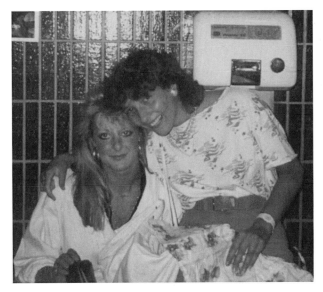

Josie's lavs

May '84

Moorfoot Tavern lavs - May '84

Life in 1980s Sheffield

'80s Sheffield

Josephines in the '80s

Josephines in the '80s

Sheffield in the '80s

Josephines

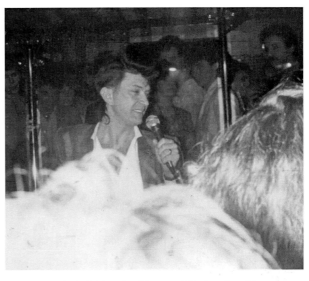

**Celeb night! Martin Shaw at Cairo Jax/Romeo
and Juliets in the '80s**

Gossips around '89

A night at Romeo's - Christmas '85

Boxing Day '84/'85 at Cairo Jax/Romeos

Chapter 6

Photoshoot Guernsey

Dear Guernsey

Thanks a million for the memories and the madness back in the 80's... oh, and the jobs!!!

Cheerie XXX

Jaki and Juliet, Oct '89, 'Golden Monkey'

'You Don't Bring Me Flowers'

A spot of shopping

My birthday, Ford Regent, Jersey

Friends

'Good 'ere init!' - Jaki and Carole
'Golden Monkey' '89

67

Waterfront workmates

Guernsey boys

Carmel Dobbins from Sheffield
and moi

You're never too old for a Friday night out

Linda and Julie - Sheffield girls

'It's a wrap'

Ravensthorpe
Victoria ter
St PP
12-11-89

Hi MARY,
Just a few lines + lots
of photos!
Well cheers for phoning
the other night ← opps day
GOSSIP →
    NIGHTLIFE — WHAT NIGHTLIFE?
    MEN   — LOTS!
    WORK   — WANK
    MONEY   — NONE
                    END OF MESSAGE!

    WRITE SOON
    TAKE CARE
            JAKI X

An early Txt Msg   Easy way of showing you photos

My Birthday Fort Regent Jersey

It's my birthday. I'm going to spend my day with my mates in Jersey. Fort Regent, 1987

The Rugby Club - the only place you could get a bevy on a Sunday - we were all regulars

Blue Dior uniform

The Guernsey American Football team with Oliver Reed RIP.
Photos kindly submitted by Mark Gilmour.

Guernsey life in the 1980s

Guernsey life in the 1980s

Guernsey life in the 1980s

Guernsey and Jersey life in the 80's

Guernsey life in the 1980s

Guernsey life in the 1980s

Guernsey life in the 1980s

Guernsey life in the 1980s

. . . .

Acknowledgements

Thanks a Million to all my friends who appear in this book. I love you all.

Lisa, Paula, Joanne, Susan and Brian are the Letter Writers, without them there would be no Lots of Love from Sheffield!

As for everyone else in the photographs, well …. Didn't we all have a lovely time the day we went to wherever?

A picture paints a thousand words!

Thank you to Angelo and Chris, the two men little and large with whom I share my life now.

Thank you to my Wonderful Mum and Dad for putting up with all my arrivals and departures from Sheffield. XX

Finally a huge Thank you to Neil Anderson, a true professional and inspirational mentor… et al.

It's a wrap!

Lots of Love

Mary…. LOL

P.S Any mistakes regarding laws, rules and regulations are all my observations and not necessarily factual.

About the Author

Mary Givens has lived and worked overseas for the majority of her life and at present she lives in Dublin. Mary works freelance as a writer and photographer. She is married with one son. This is her first book.